Car and Truck Show Coloring Book
25 Grayscale Cars and Trucks

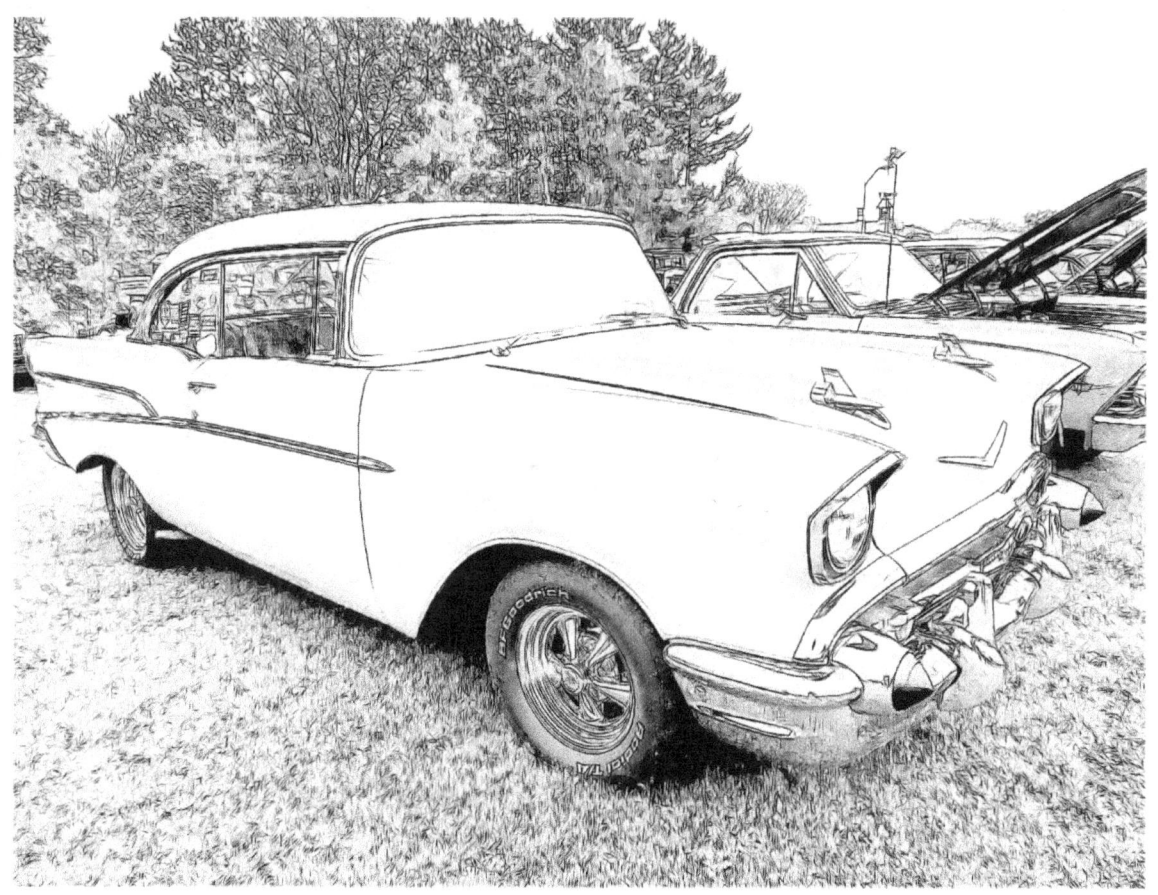

Adult Coloring Book

GRACE BRANNIGAN

Photographs Elaine Warfield

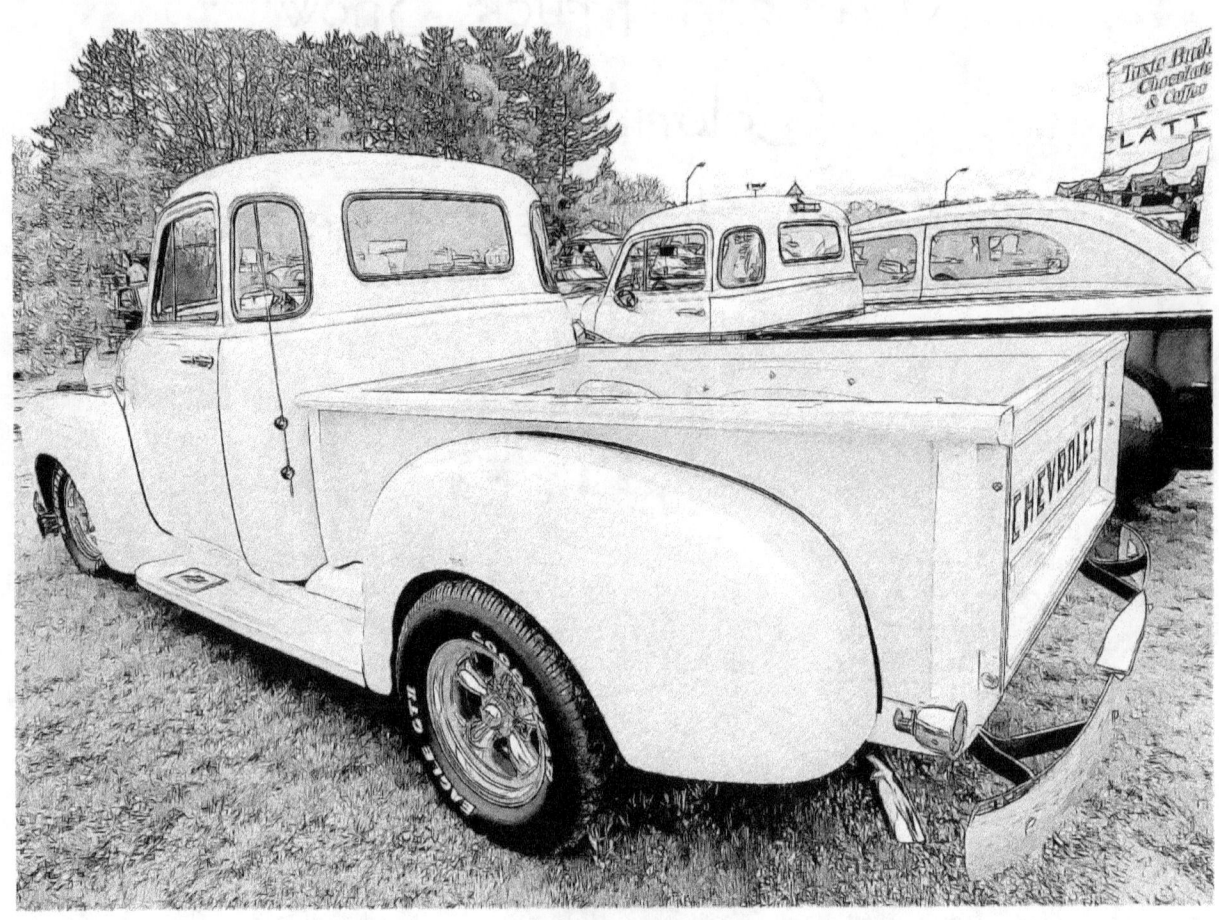

Author Website: http://www.ColoringBooksForAdults.info
Car and Truck Show Coloring Book
Copyright 2016 Elaine Warfield
ISBN-13: 978-1534761483
ISBN-10: 1534761489

Please check out my other coloring books:
Detailed Mandala Coloring Books 1 through 4
Detailed Alphabet Coloring Book: 25 Baroque Grayscale Images
Renaissance Masks: 25 Grayscale Images
On the Go Pocket Size Coloring Books
Fairies in the Garden
Be My Valentine: Vintage Valentines to Color
Scenic Catskill Mountains: 25 Photographs to Color
Plus 20+ sketchbooks and journals

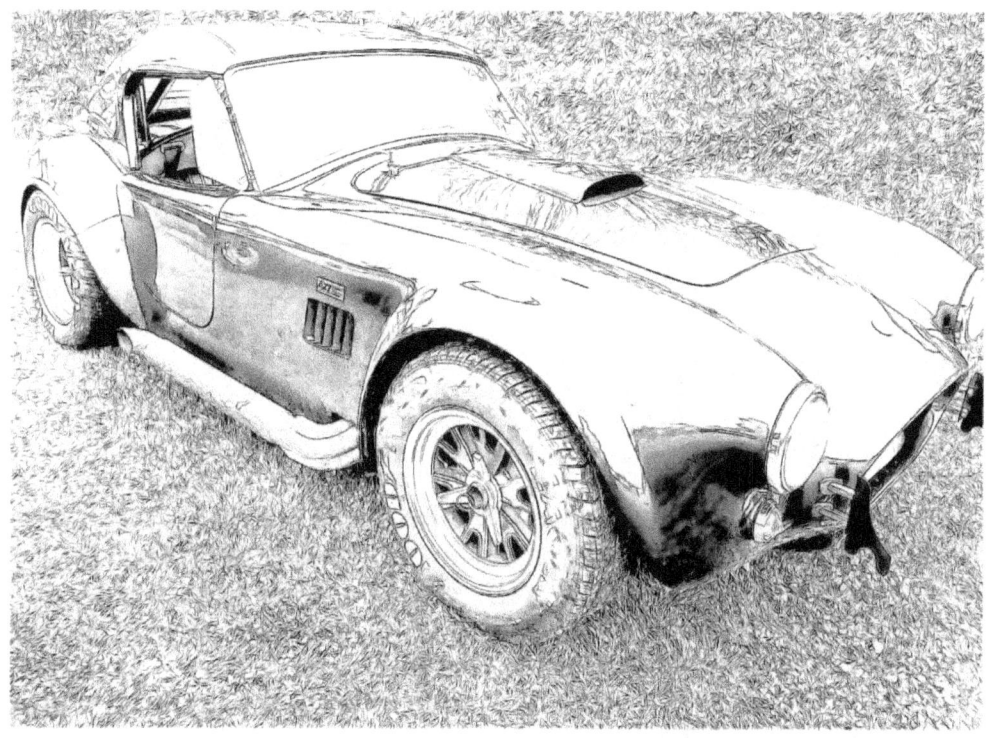

This coloring book has 25 Grayscale images which have been created as photographs copyrighted by Elaine Warfield, and manipulated by computer into grayscale images for your coloring pleasure! To give you the optimum coloring experience, most of the images have been rotated to give you the largest space to color! **As a colorist you can post these images once colored, but under copyright law you cannot claim any copyright to these images or use any copyright symbols in relation to these images.**

∞ ∞ ∞ ∞ ∞ ∞ ∞ ∞ ∞ ∞ ∞ ∞ ∞ ∞ ∞ ∞ ∞

How to Color Grayscale: Coloring *Grayscale* images is a fun way to explore and color and it makes shading easier to learn when you follow the shading already in the images. The end result is a uniquely rich and rewarding colored image. The cover for this book was colored using permanent markers, gel pens and watercolor pencils. Experiment, have fun! Please visit Grace Branngan Author Youtube channel for short videos on coloring grayscale.

Coloring has been shown to reduce stress and offer meditative release. Create your own visually appealing art using crayons, colored pencils, felt tip markers, ink pens, art pencils, gel pens, glitter pens. There is no limit to your creativity and genius.

Please leave a review where you bought this coloring book and share your coloring images. It really helps the author and other buyers. Please check out my other coloring books and visit my Facebook page **Coloring Books for Adults Info.**

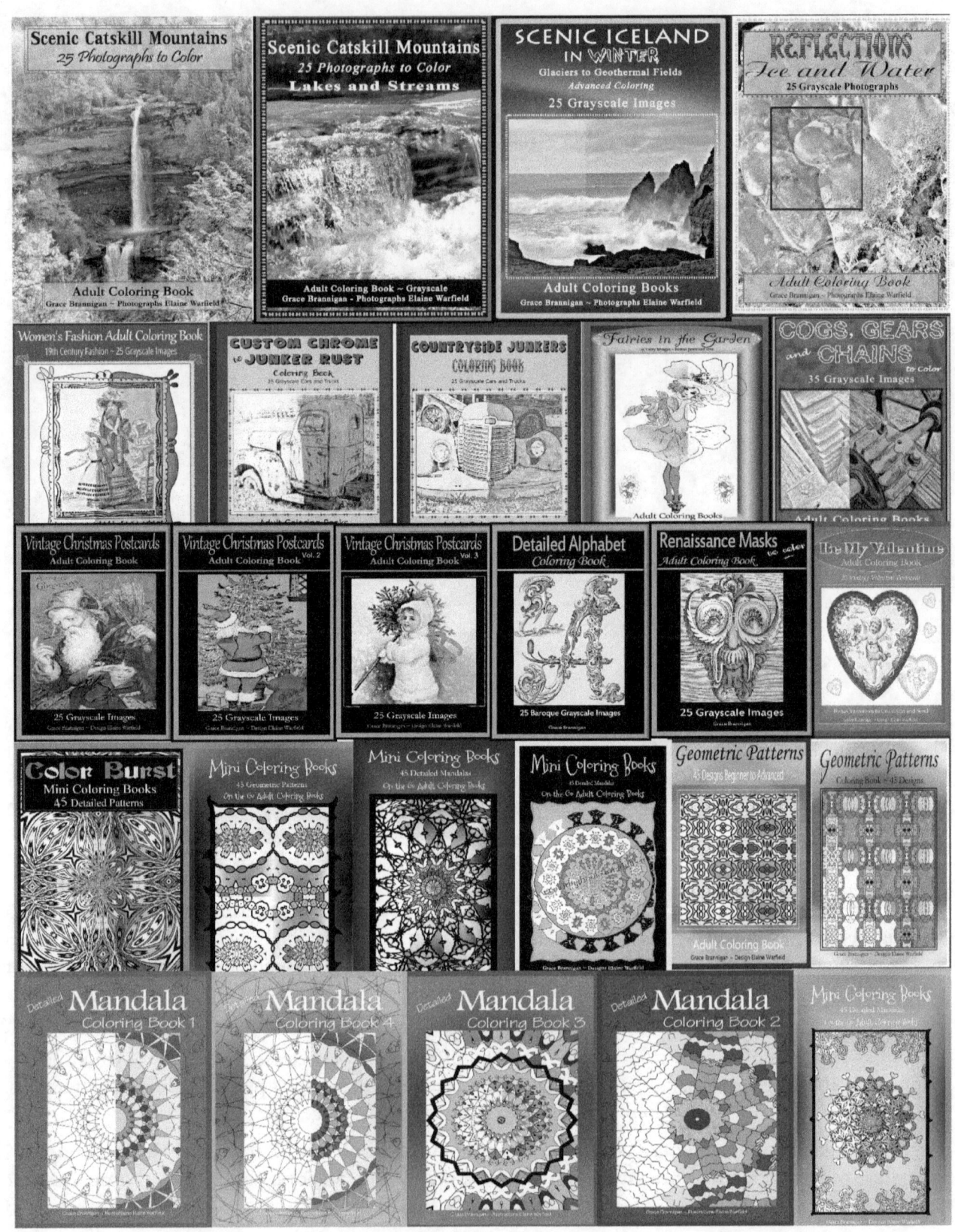

Color, Color, Color!

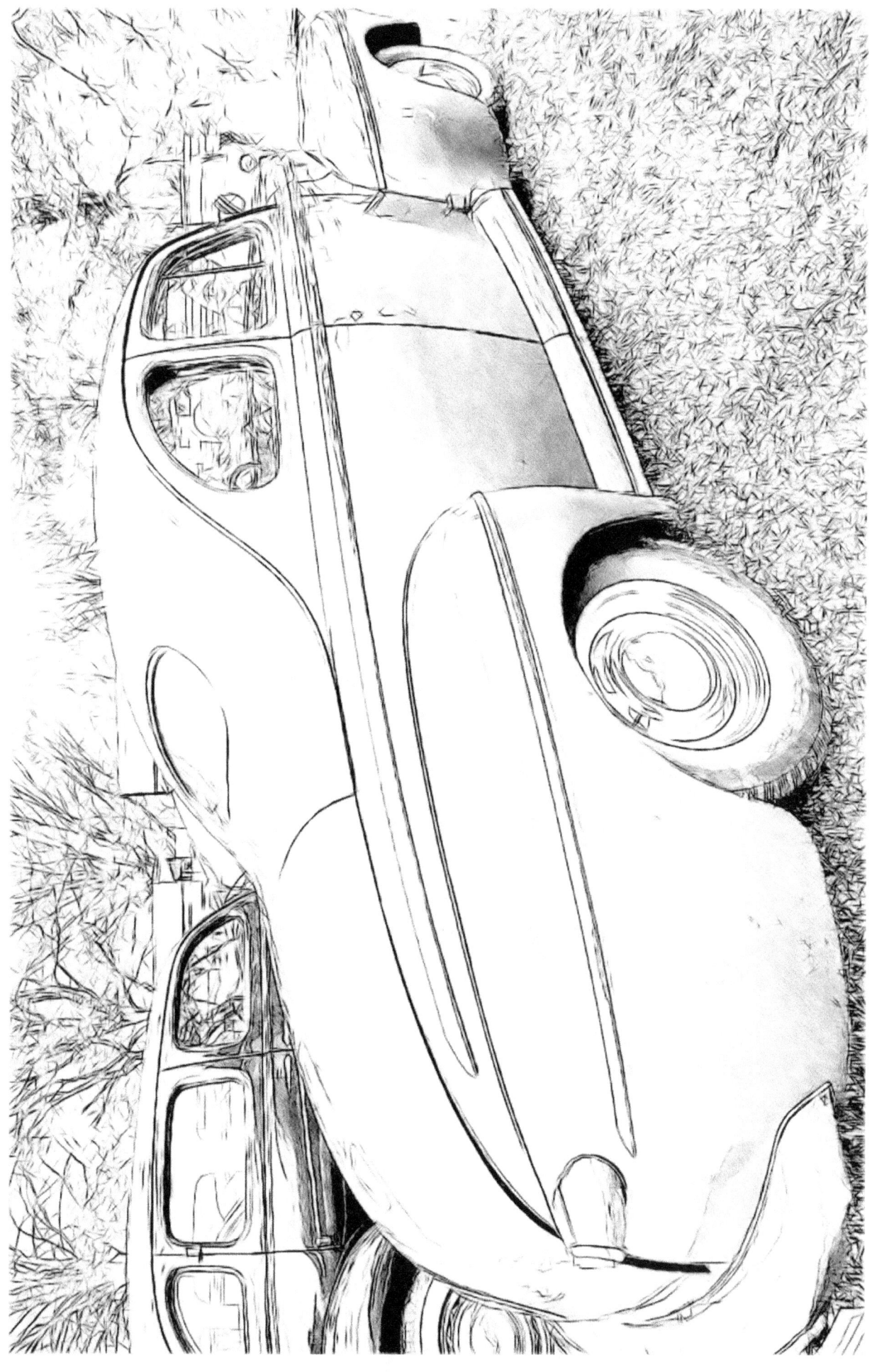

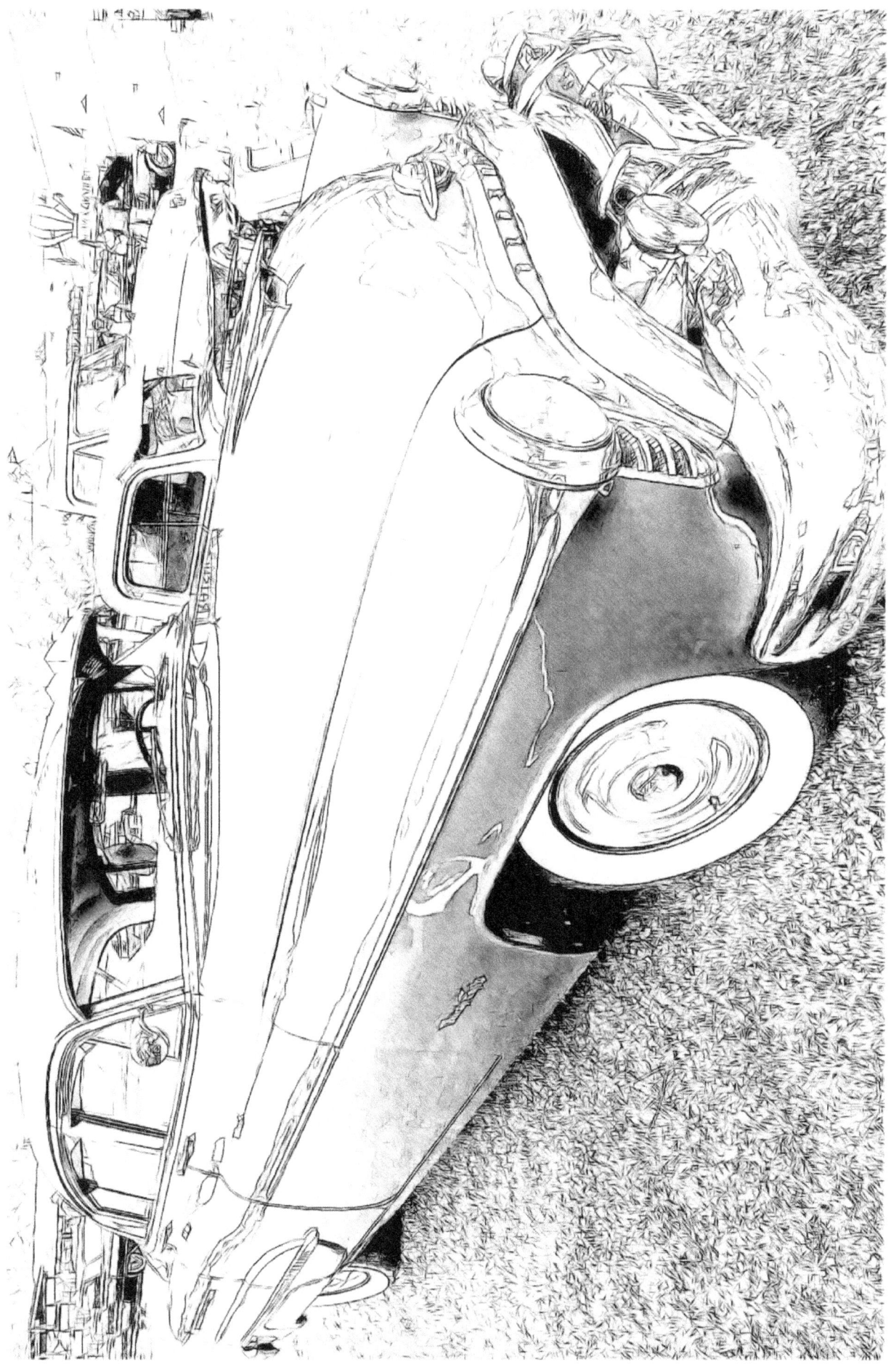

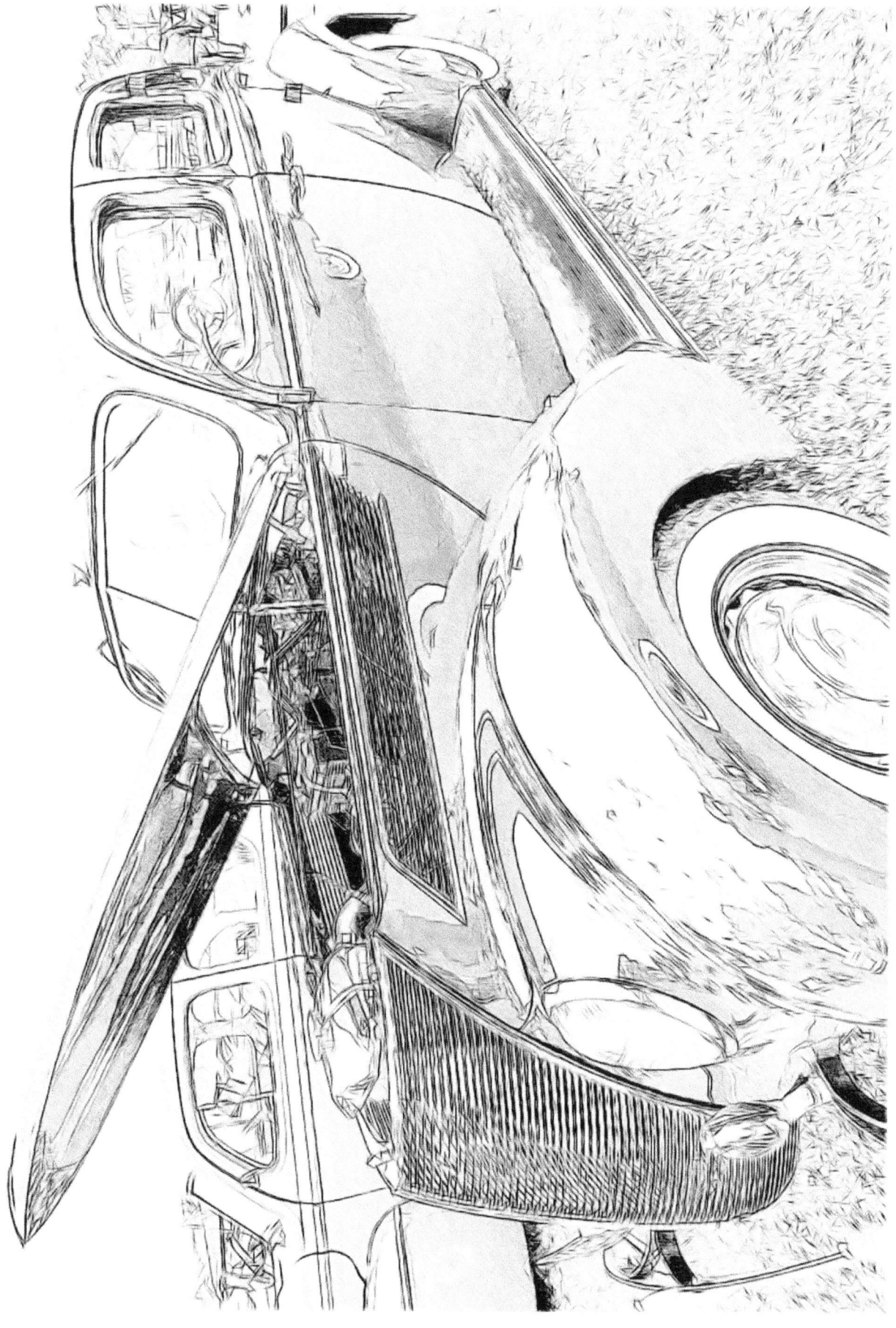

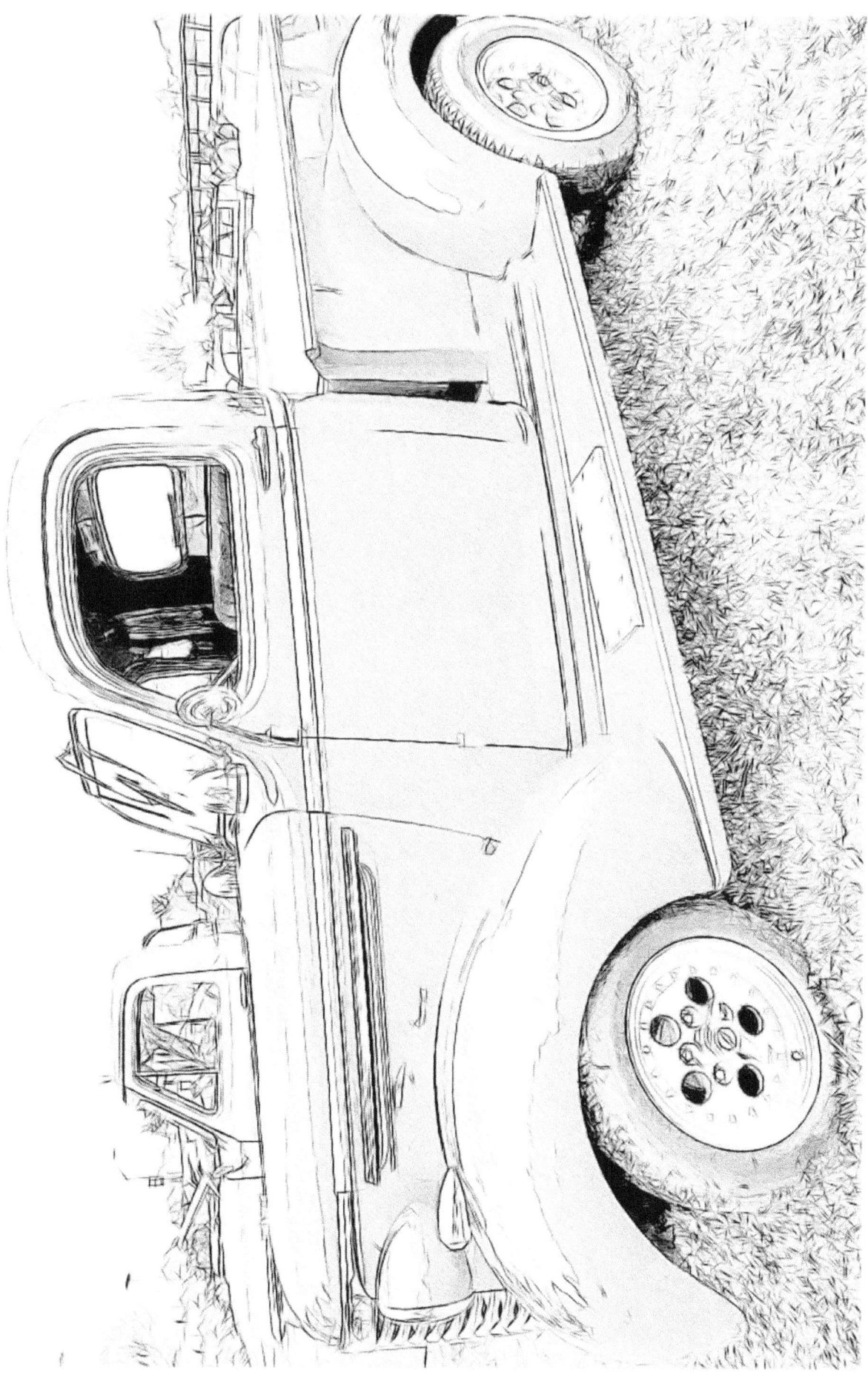

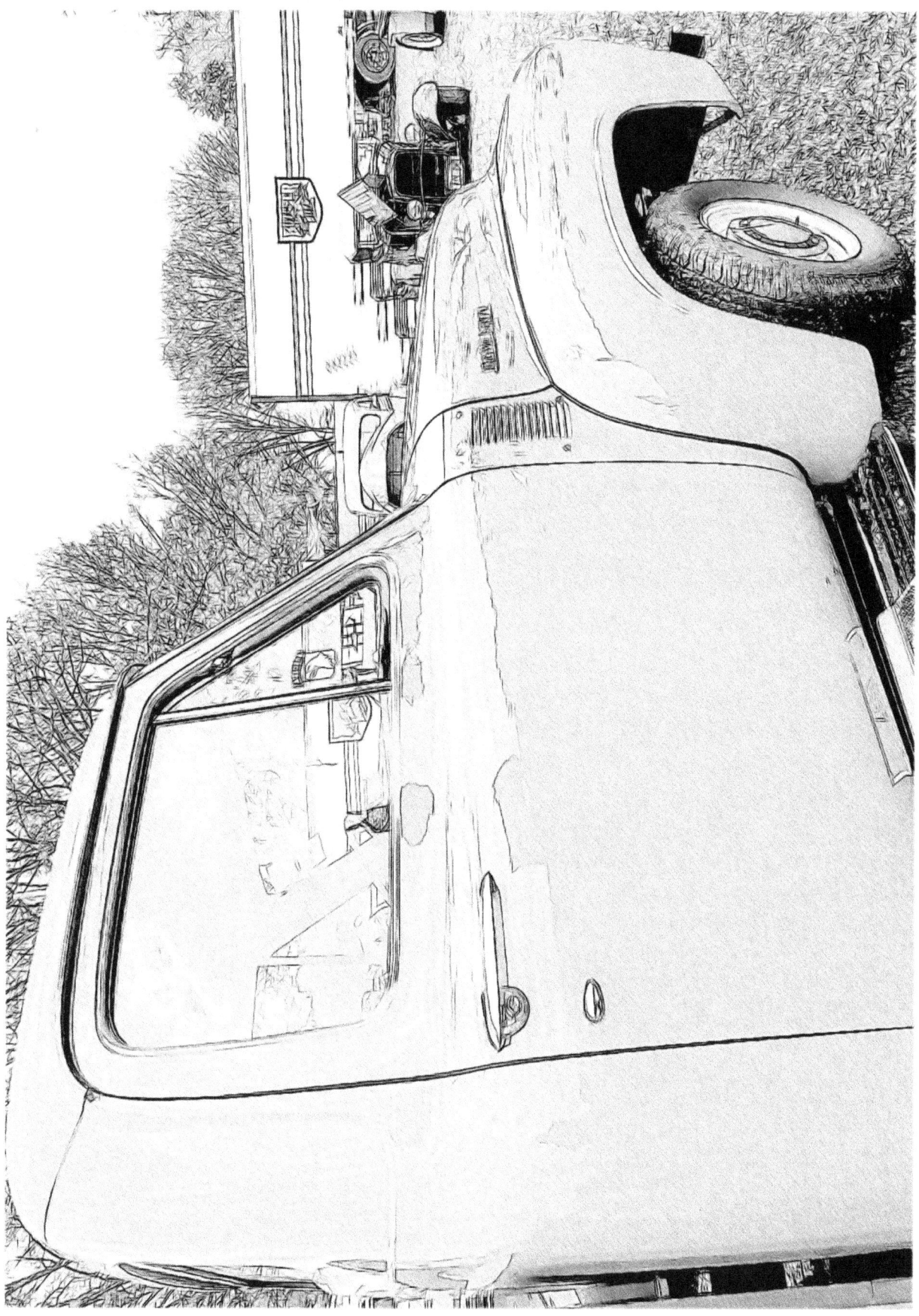

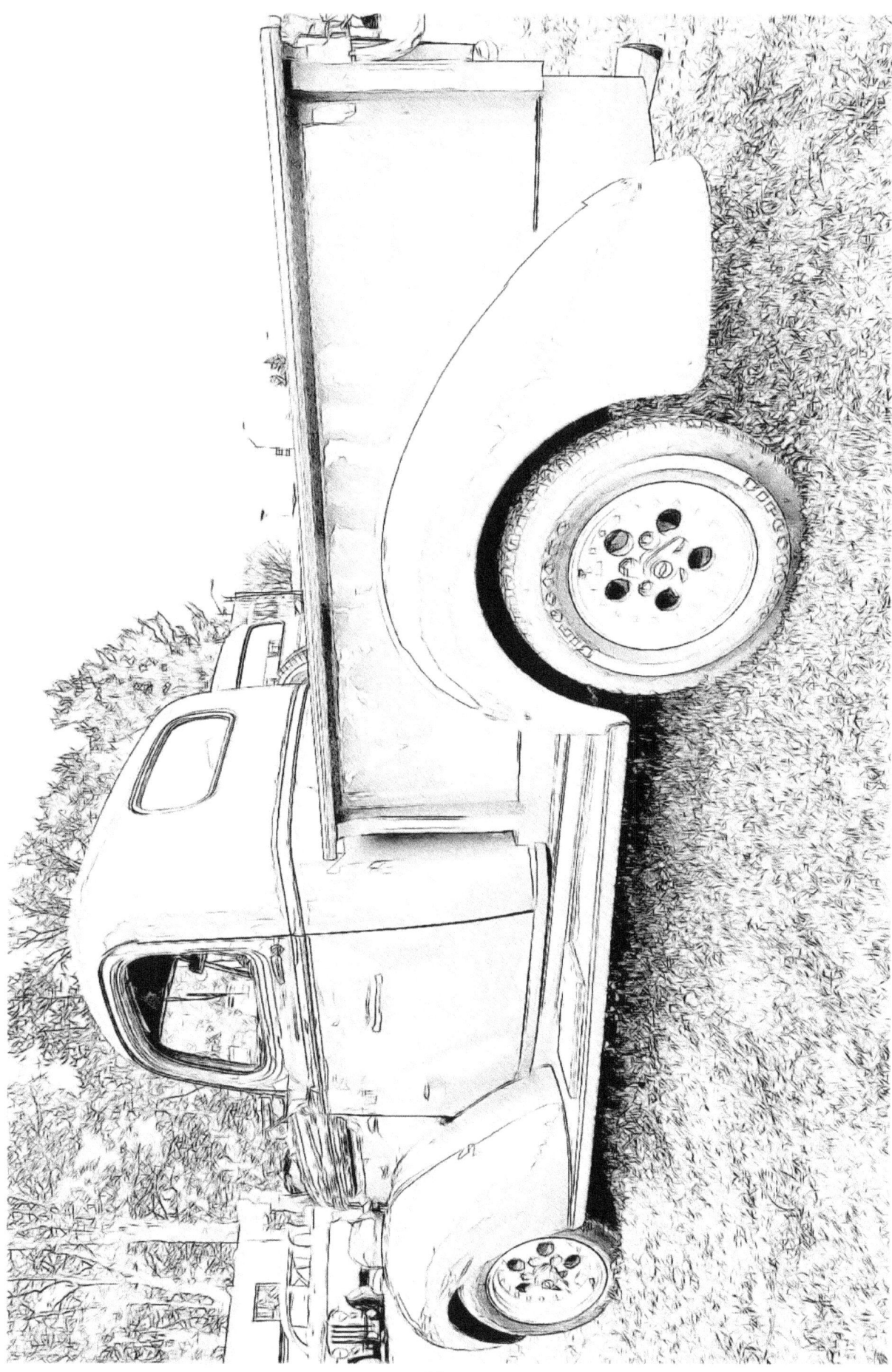

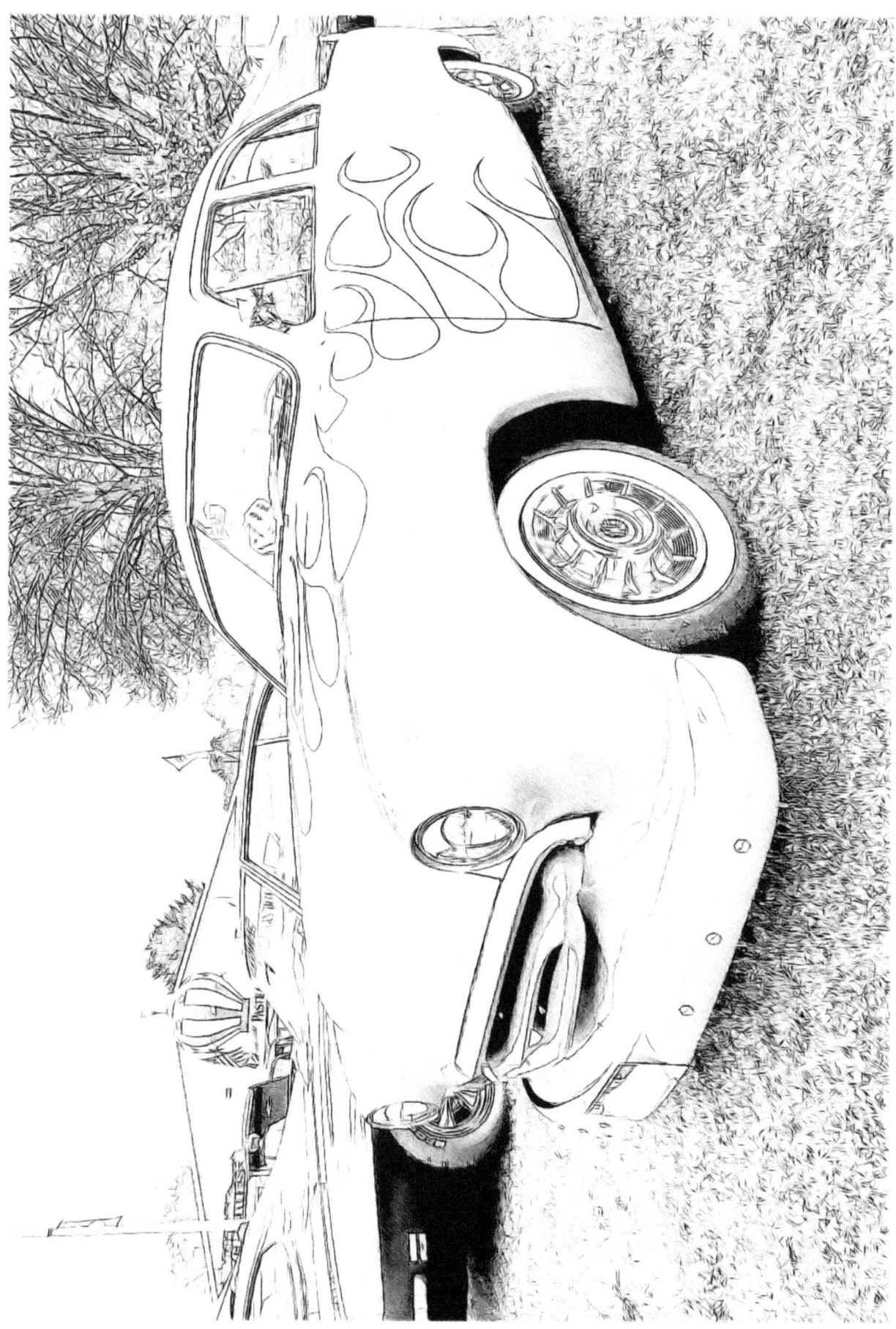

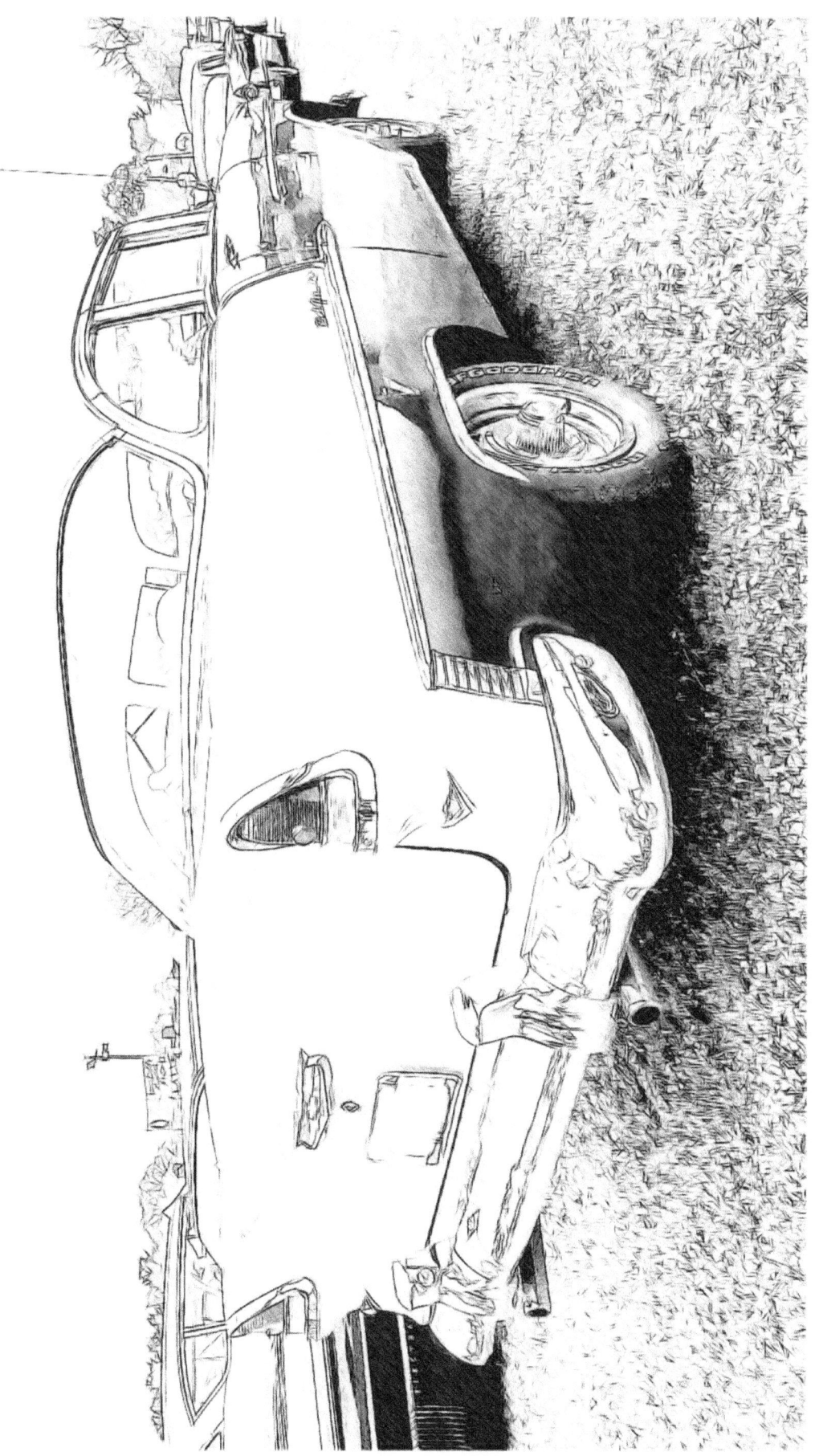

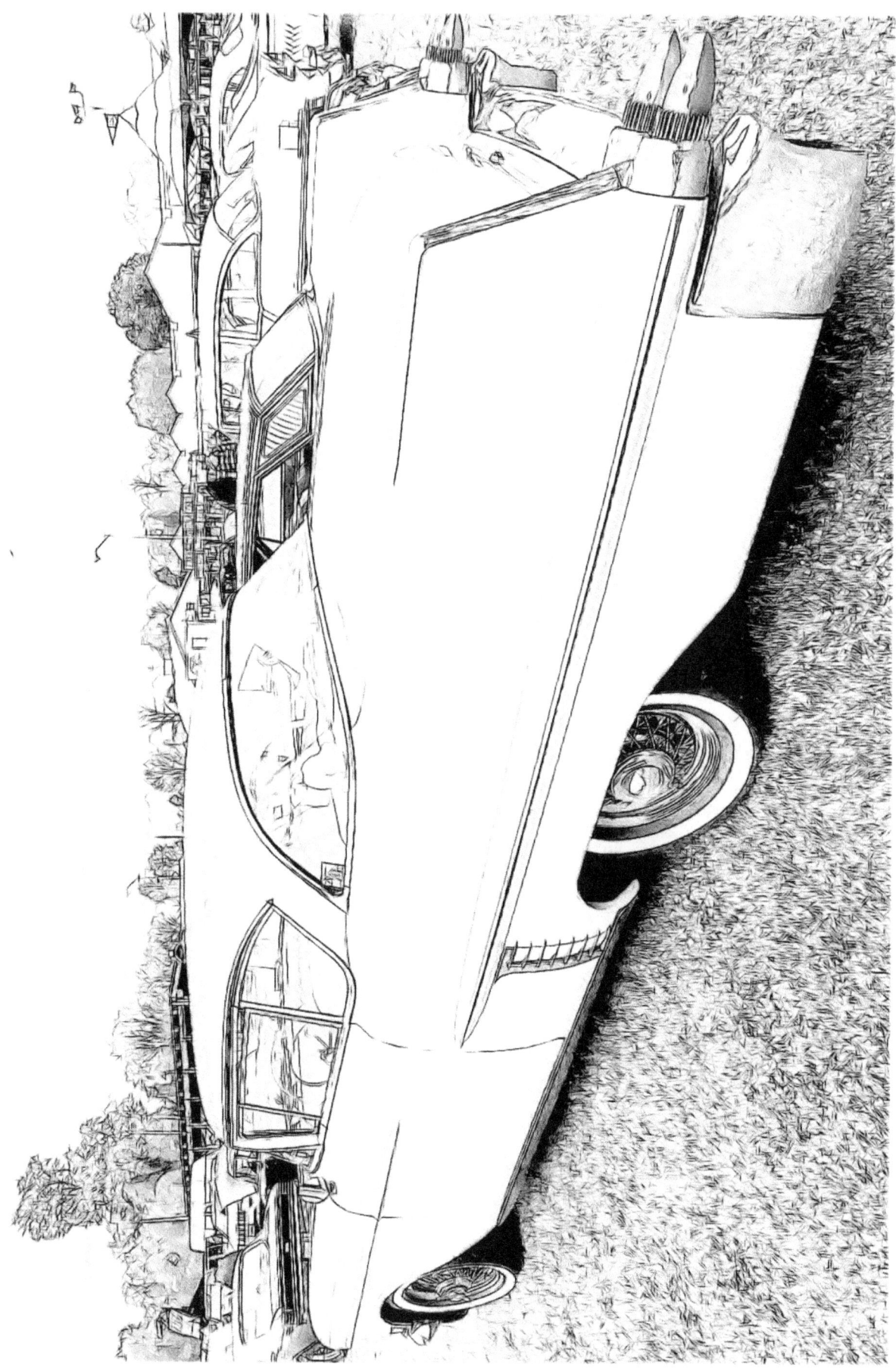

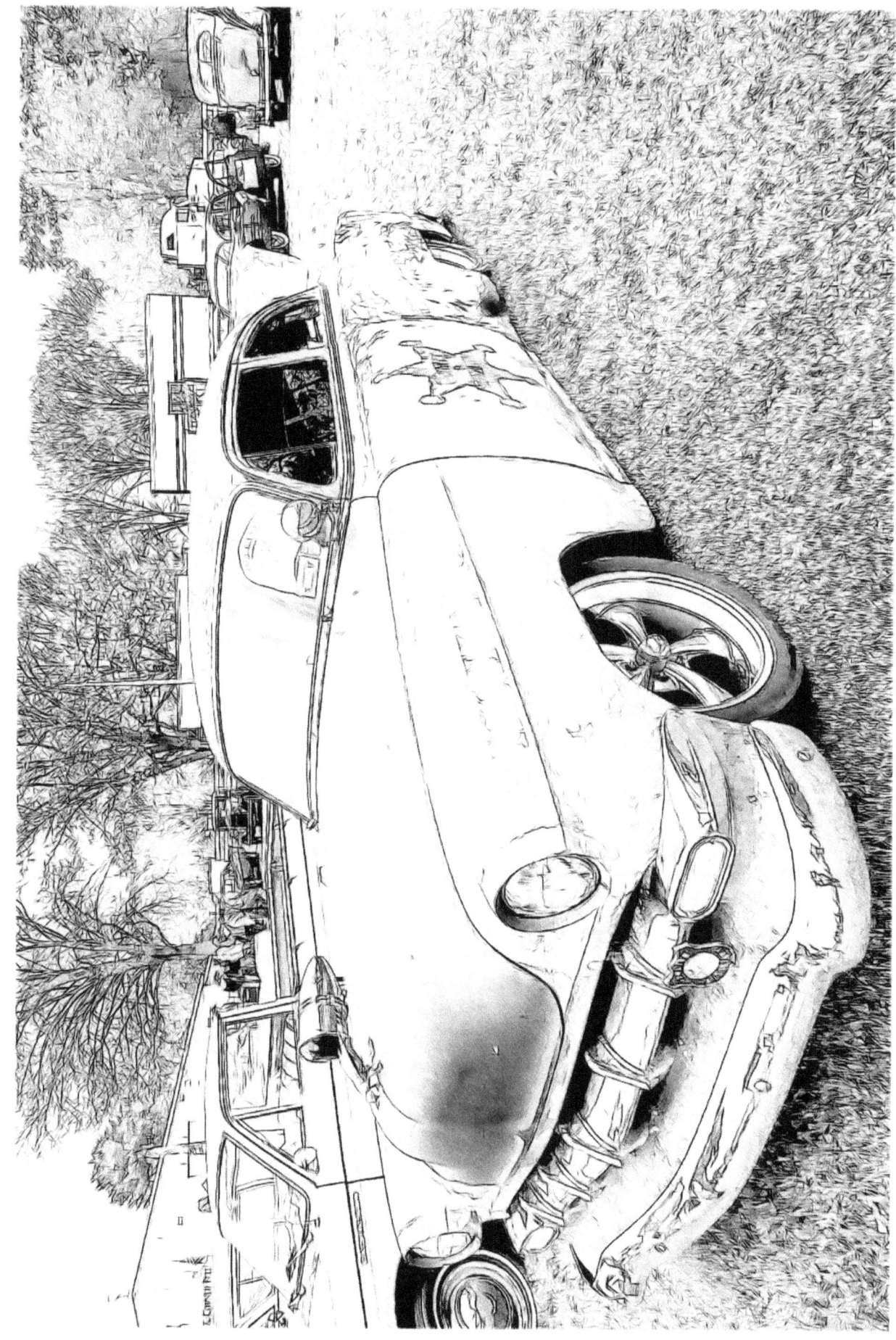

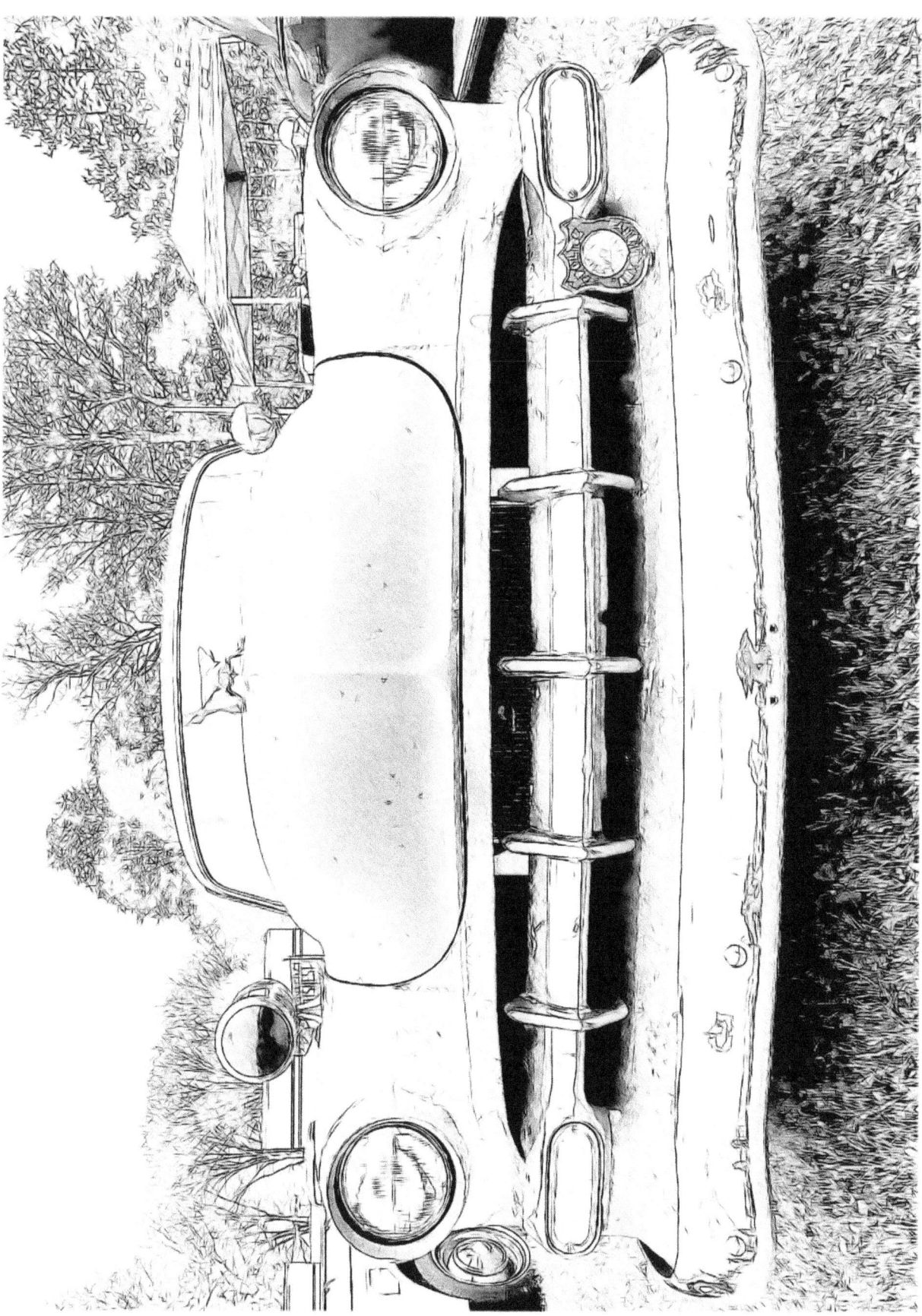

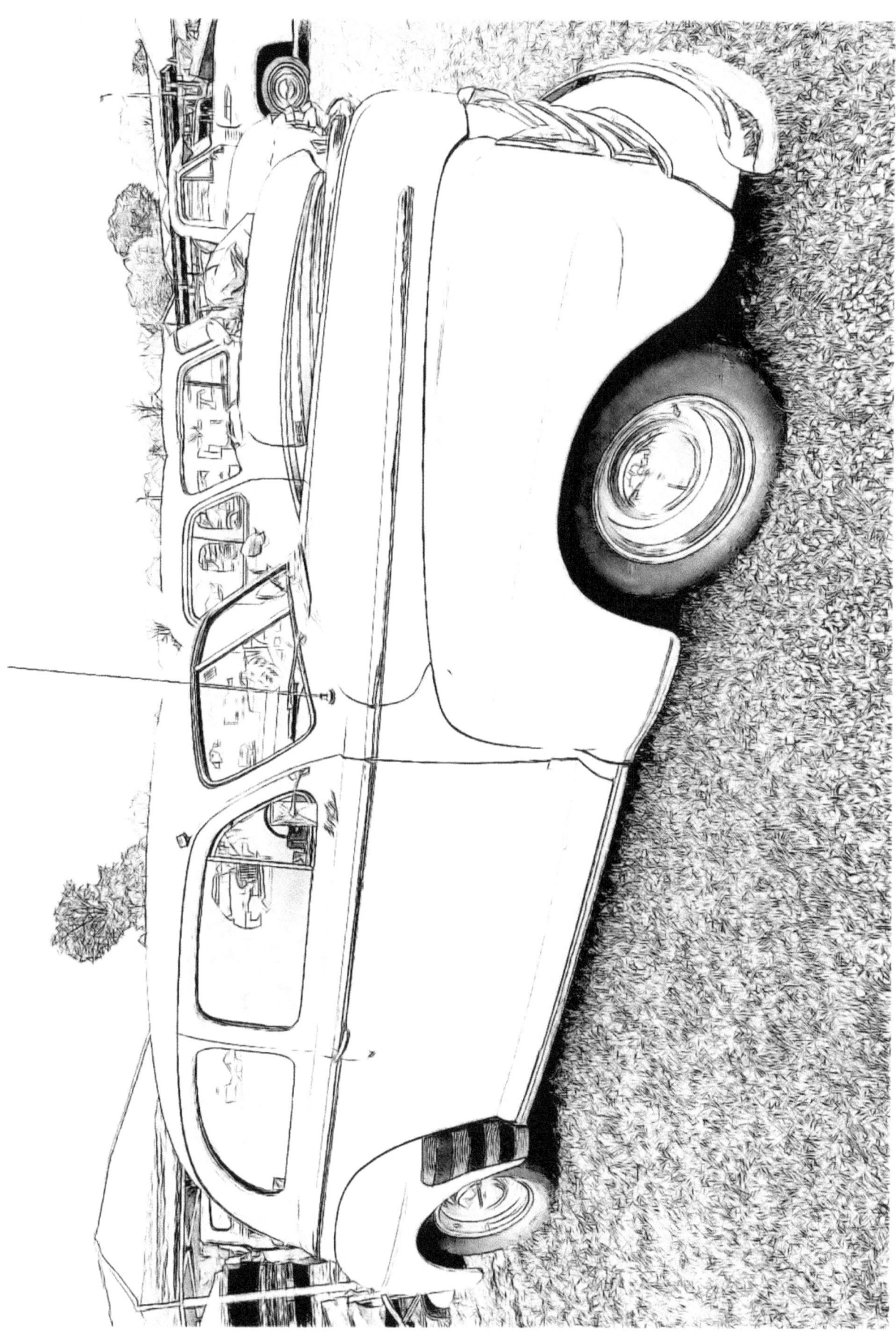

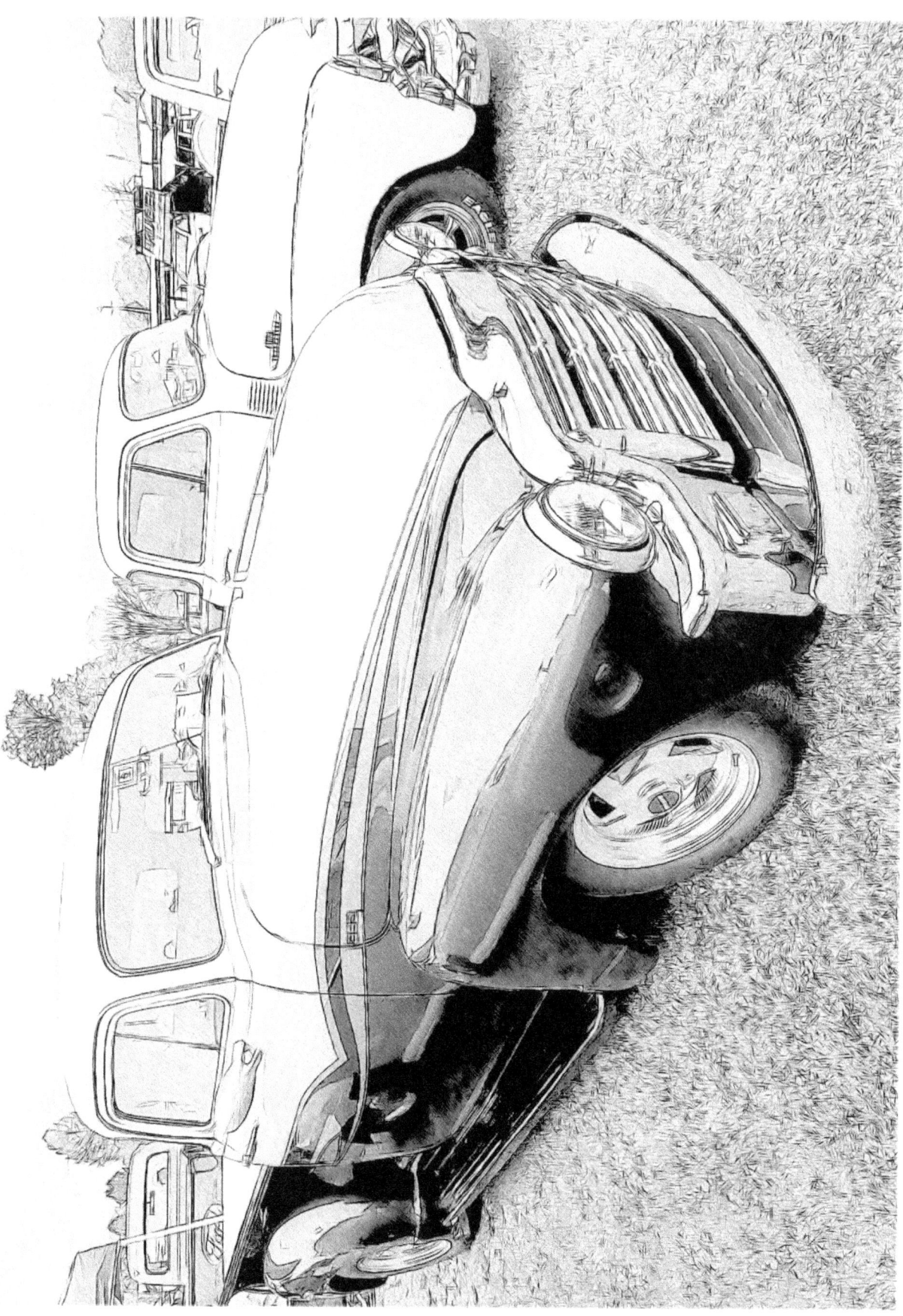

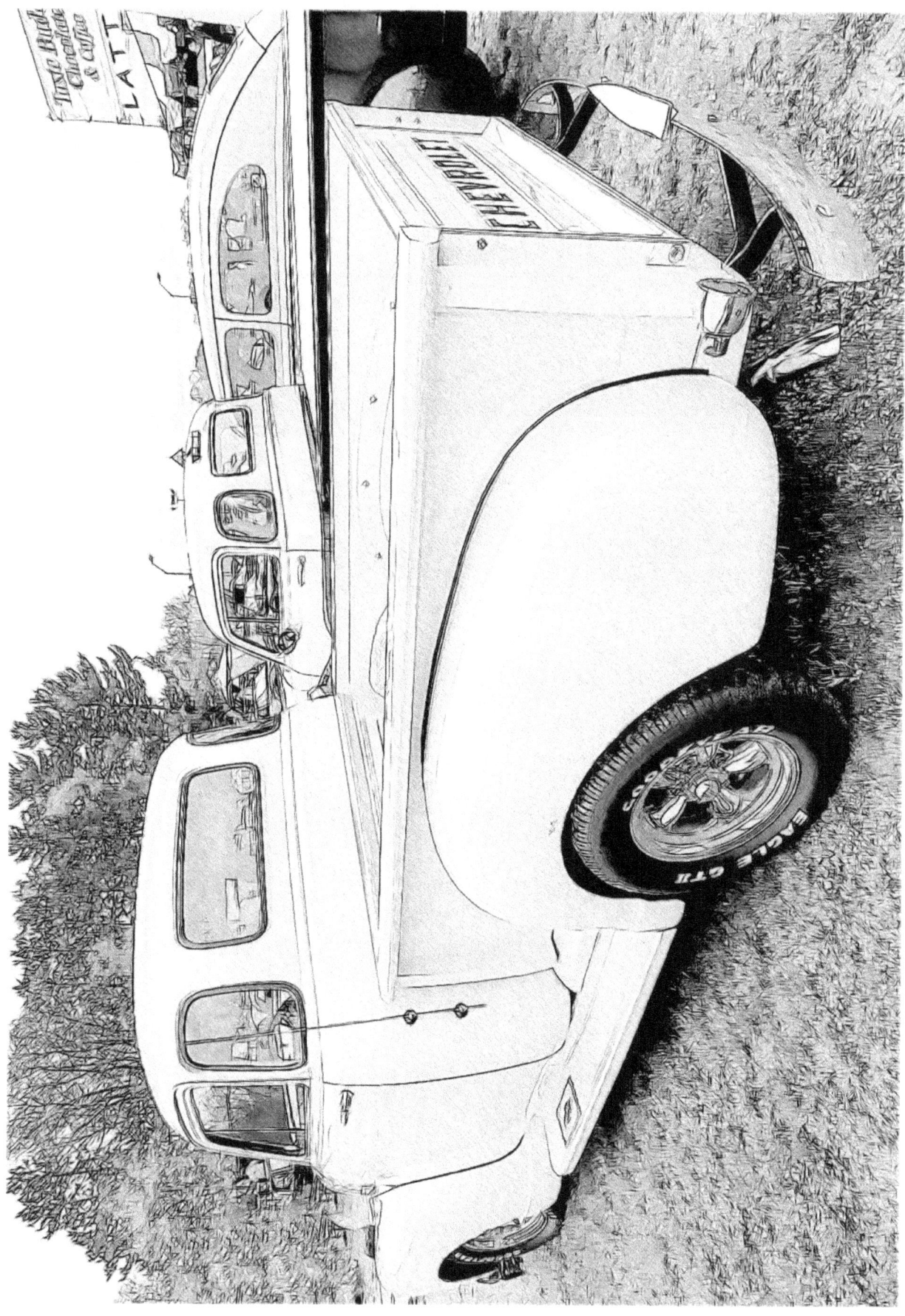

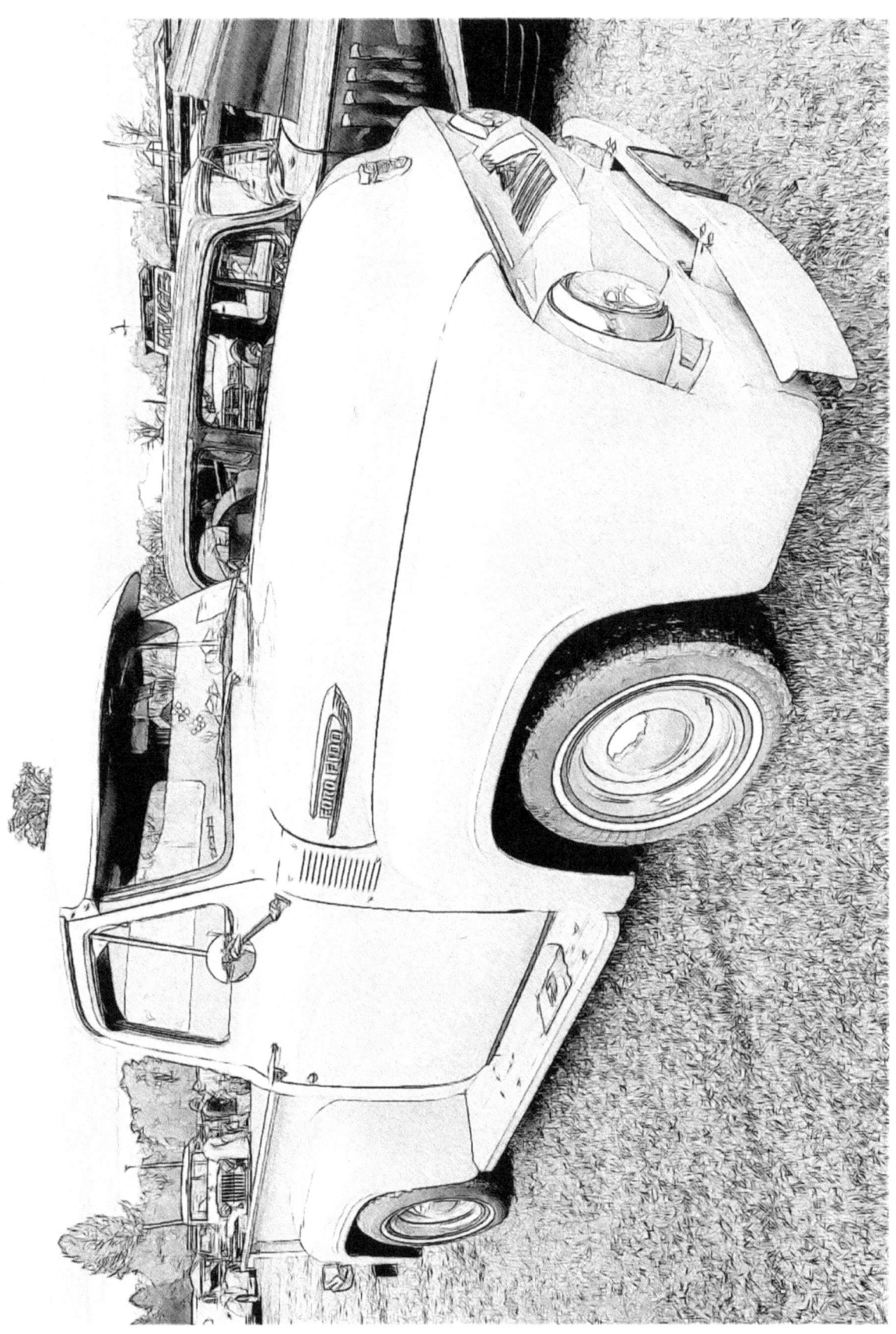

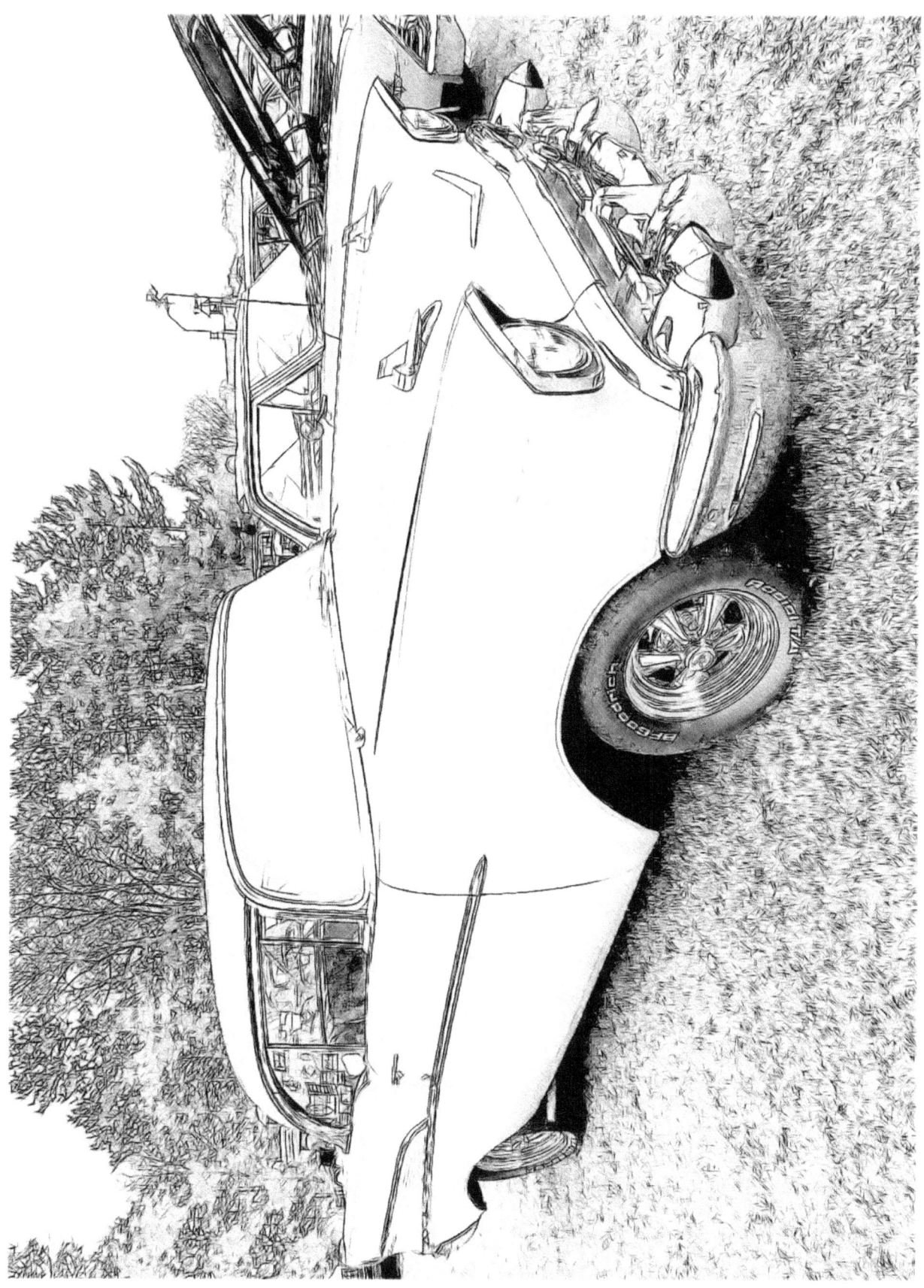

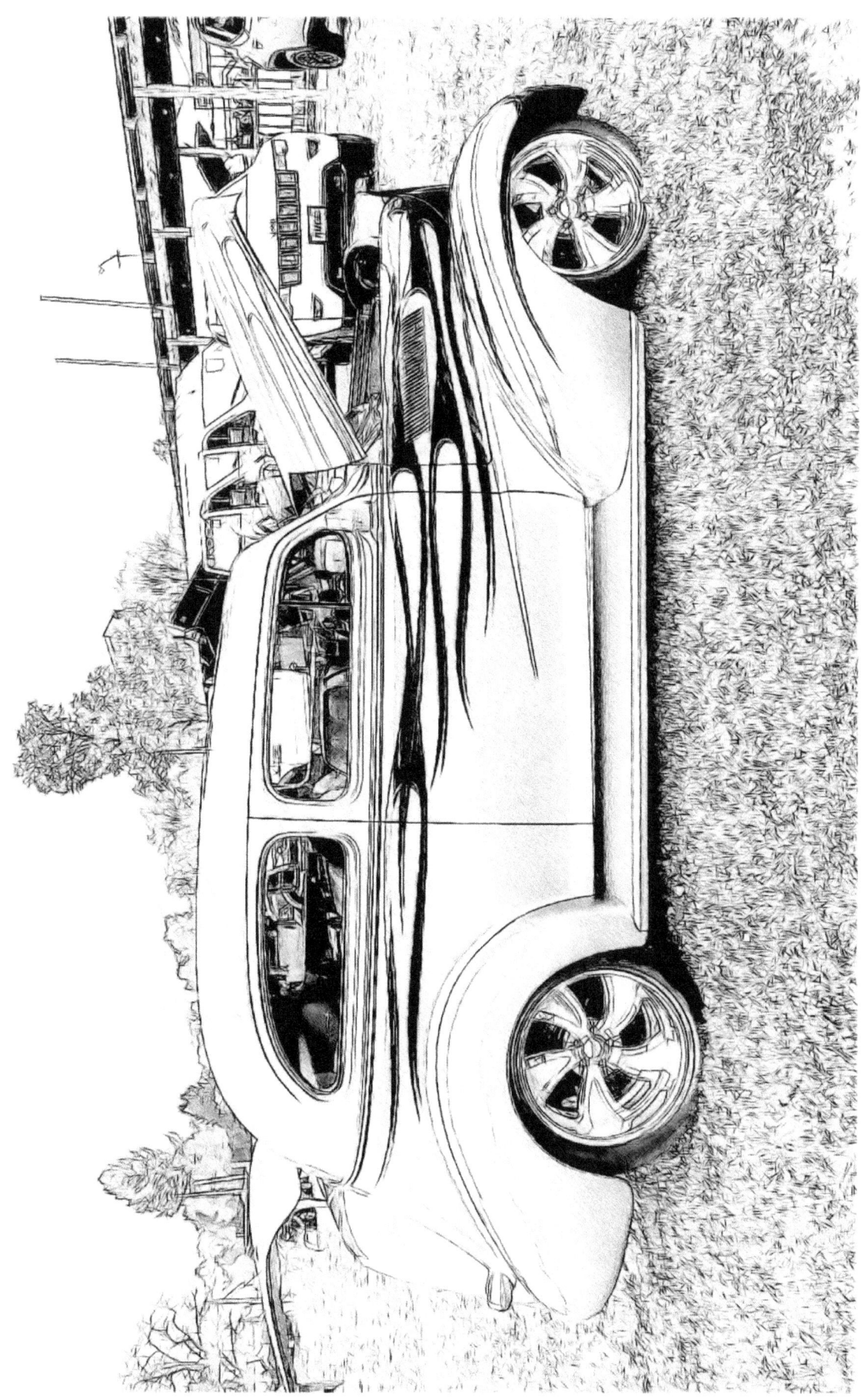

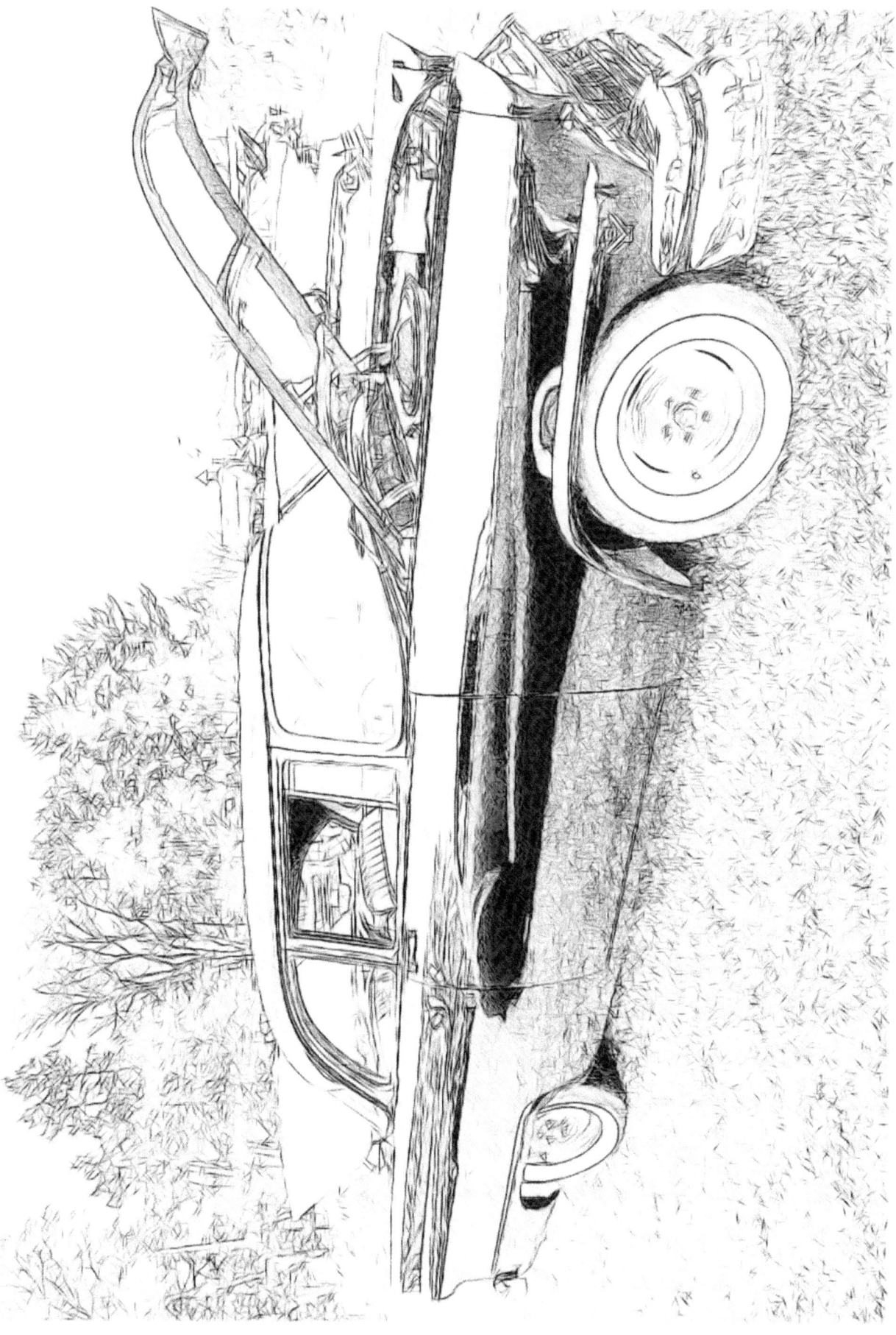

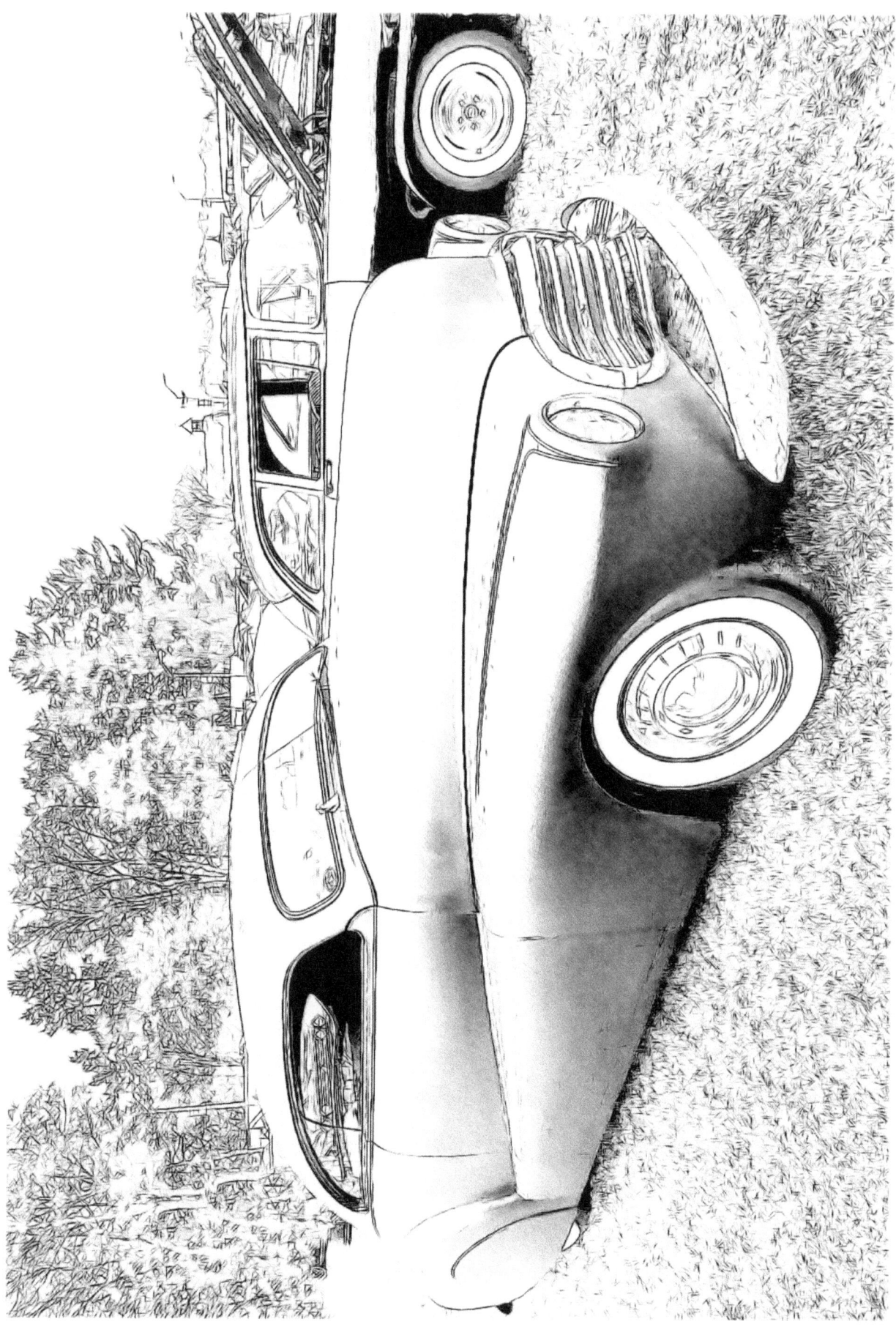

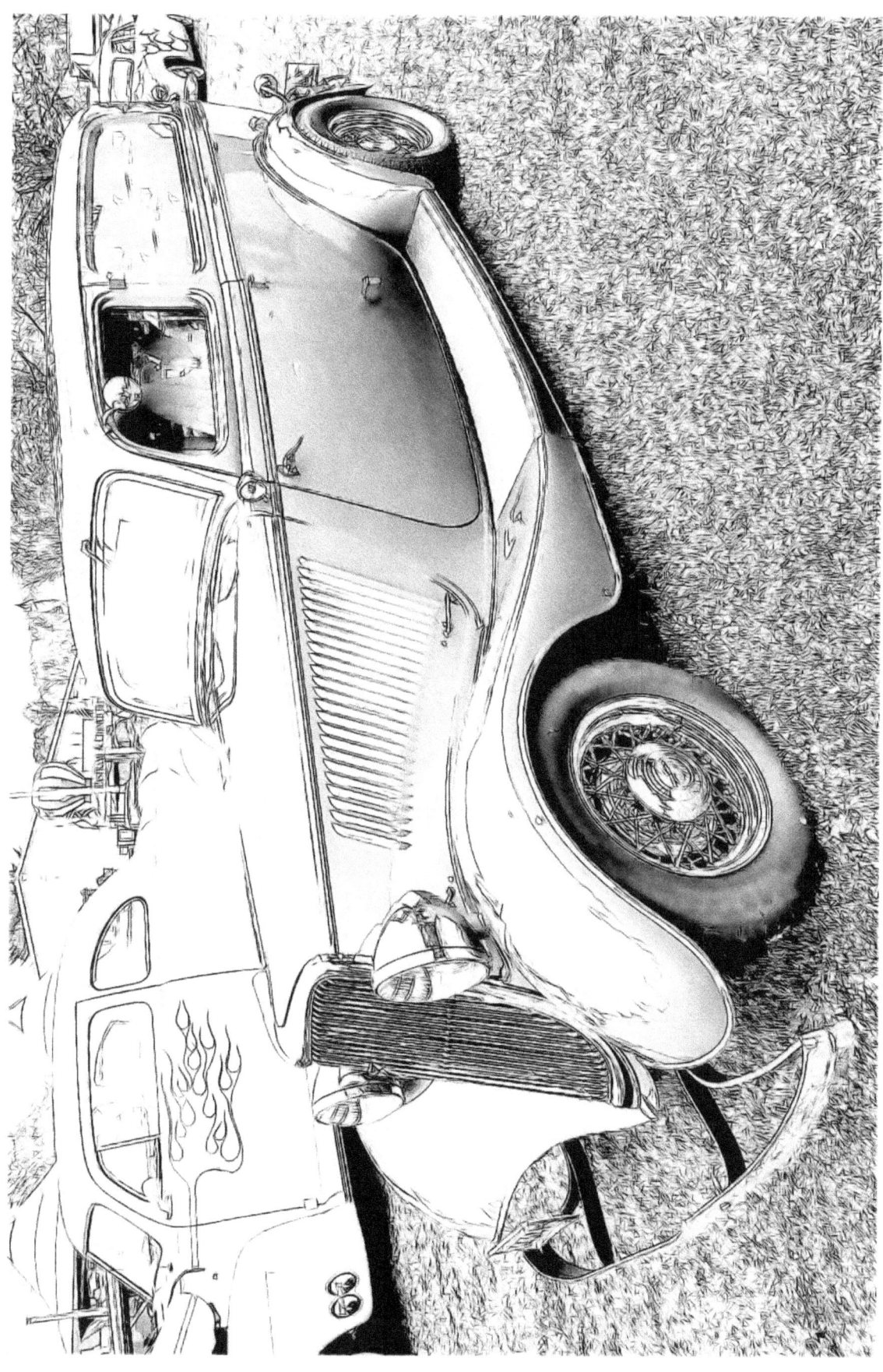

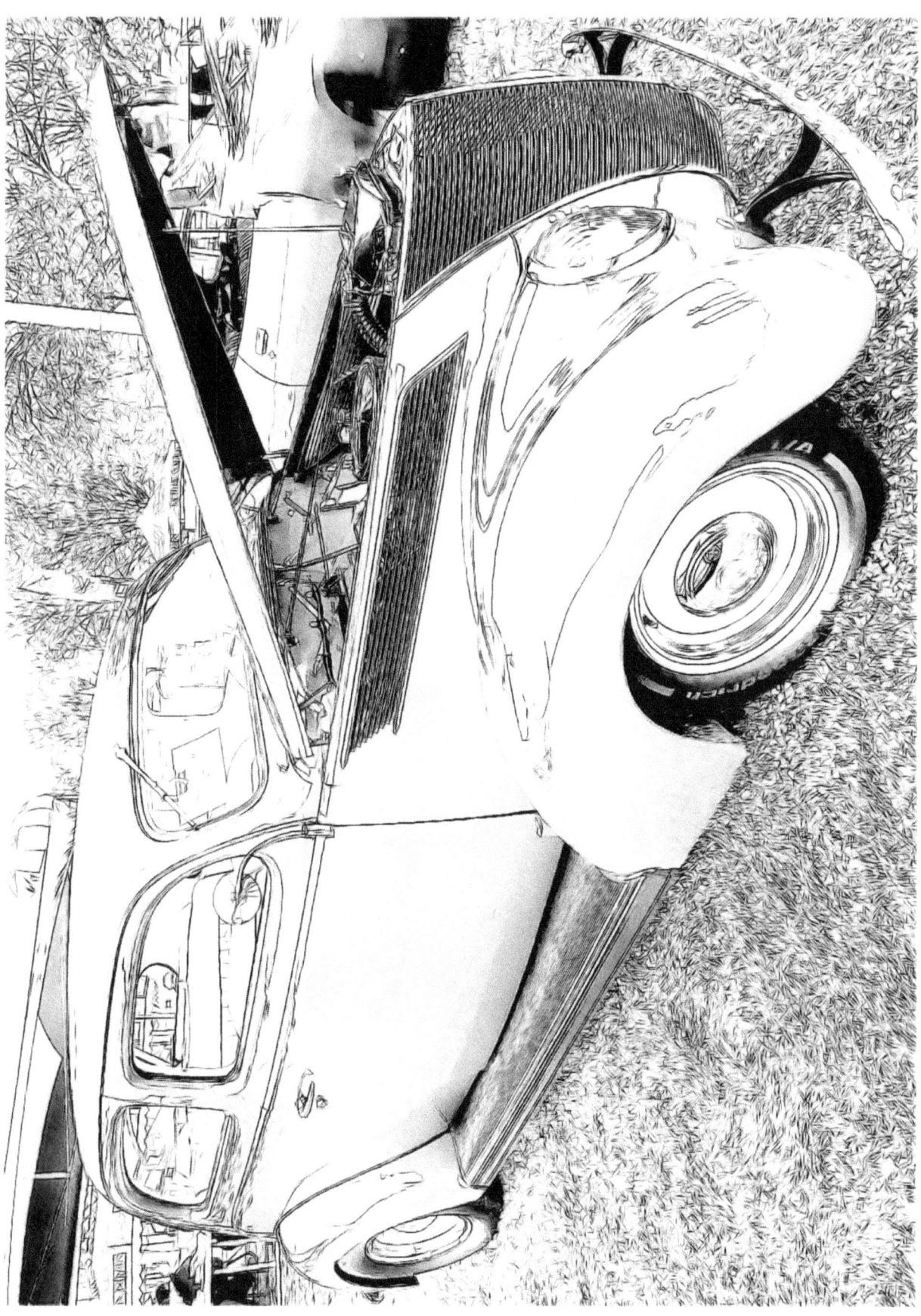

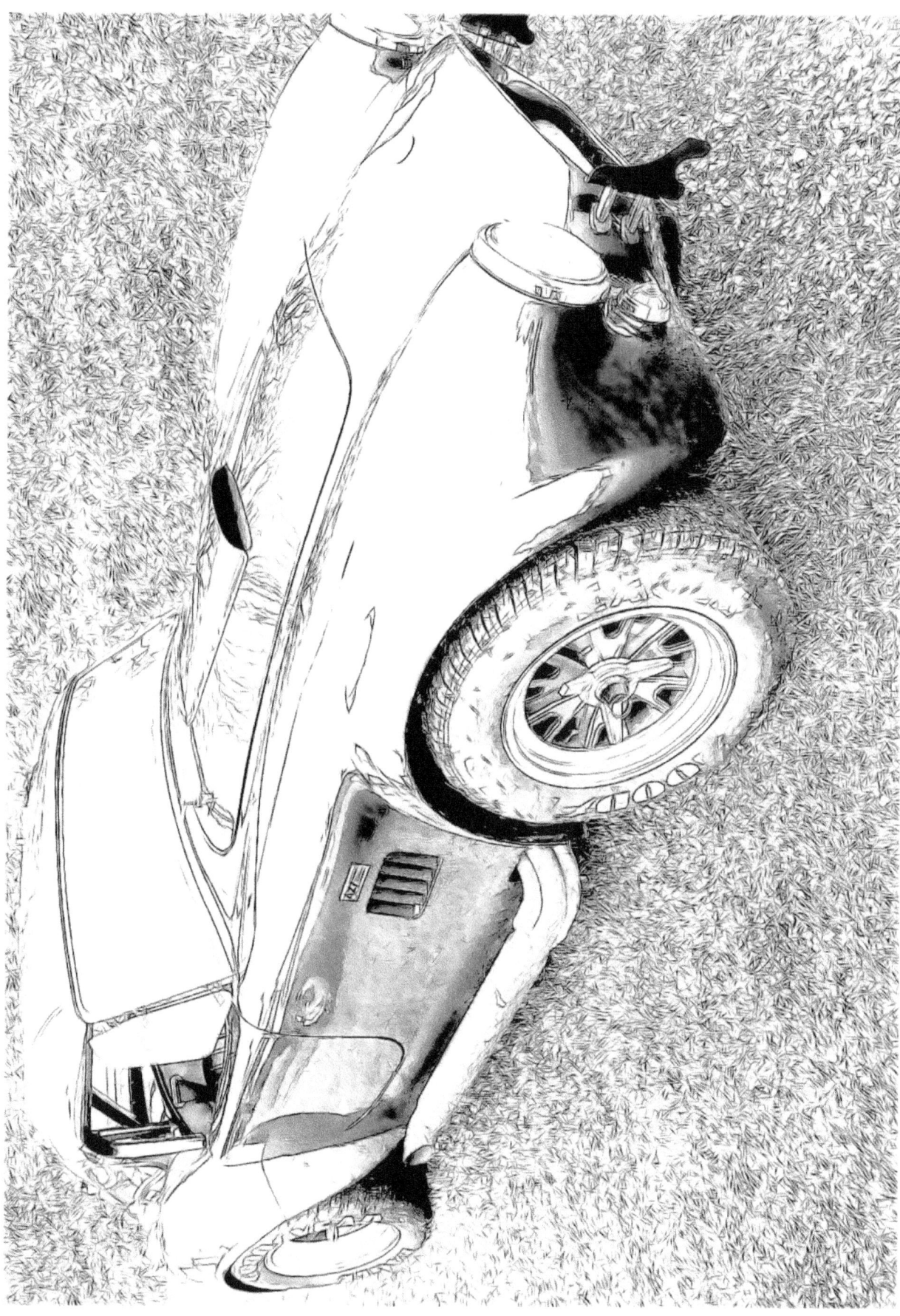

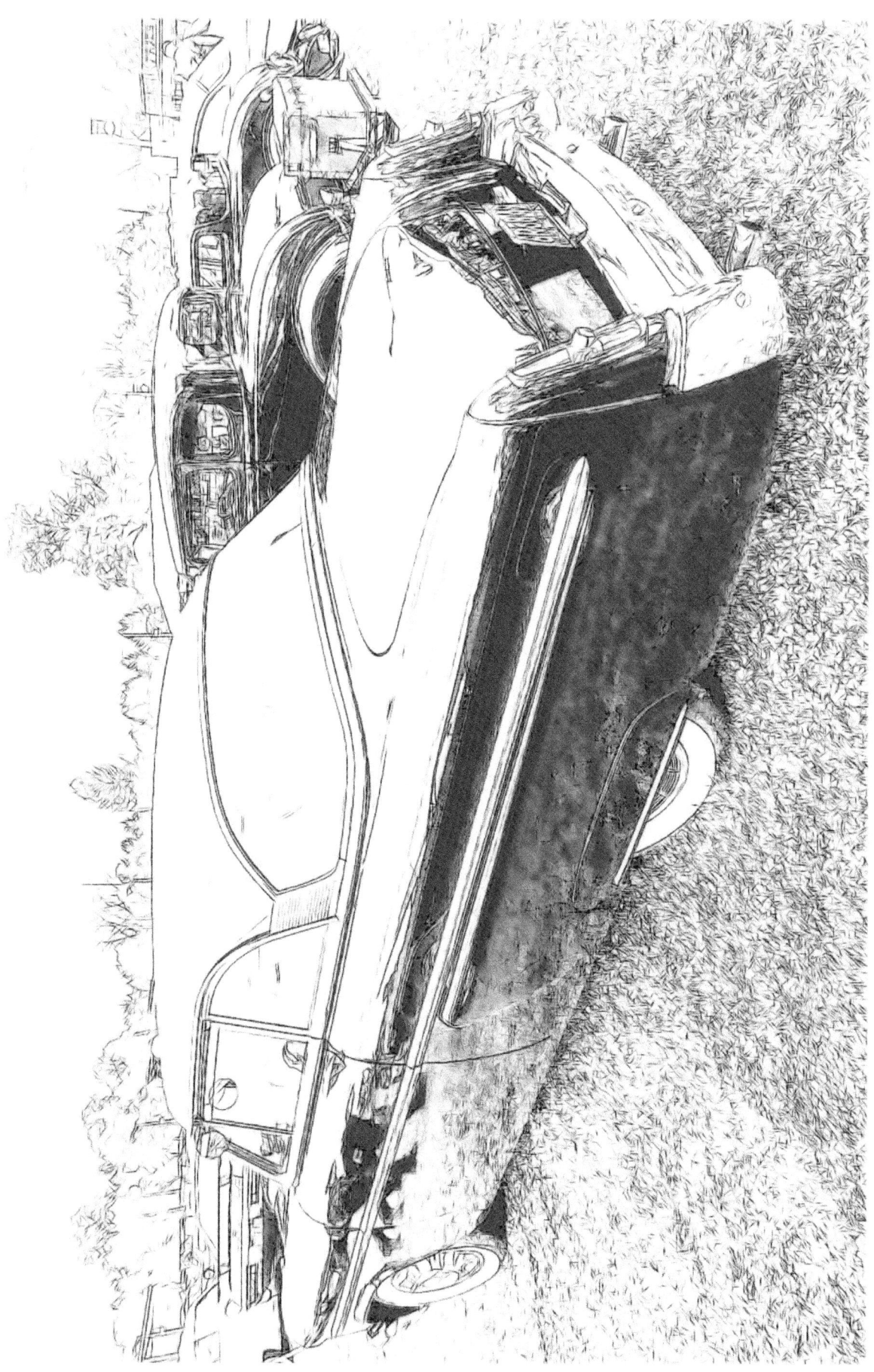

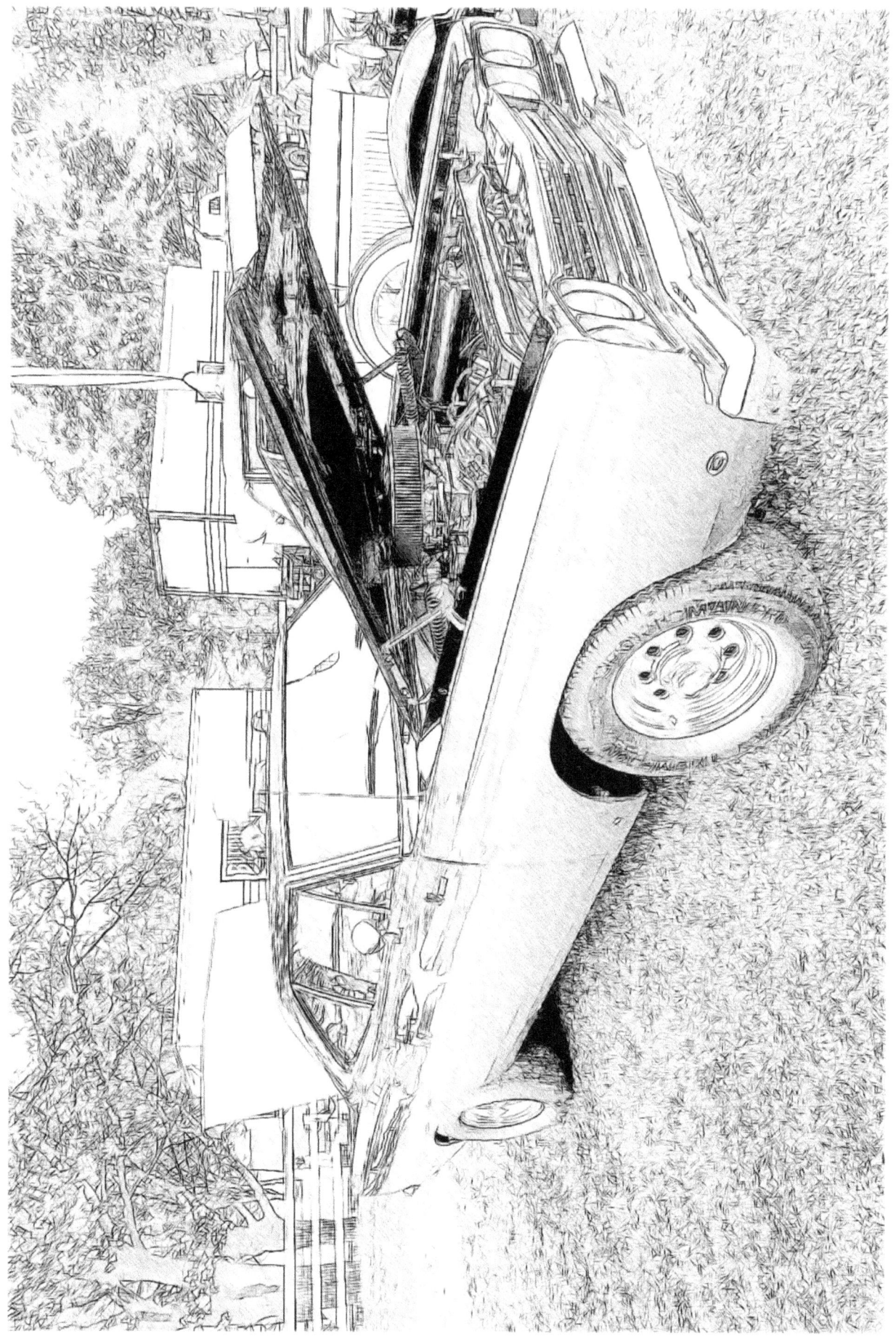

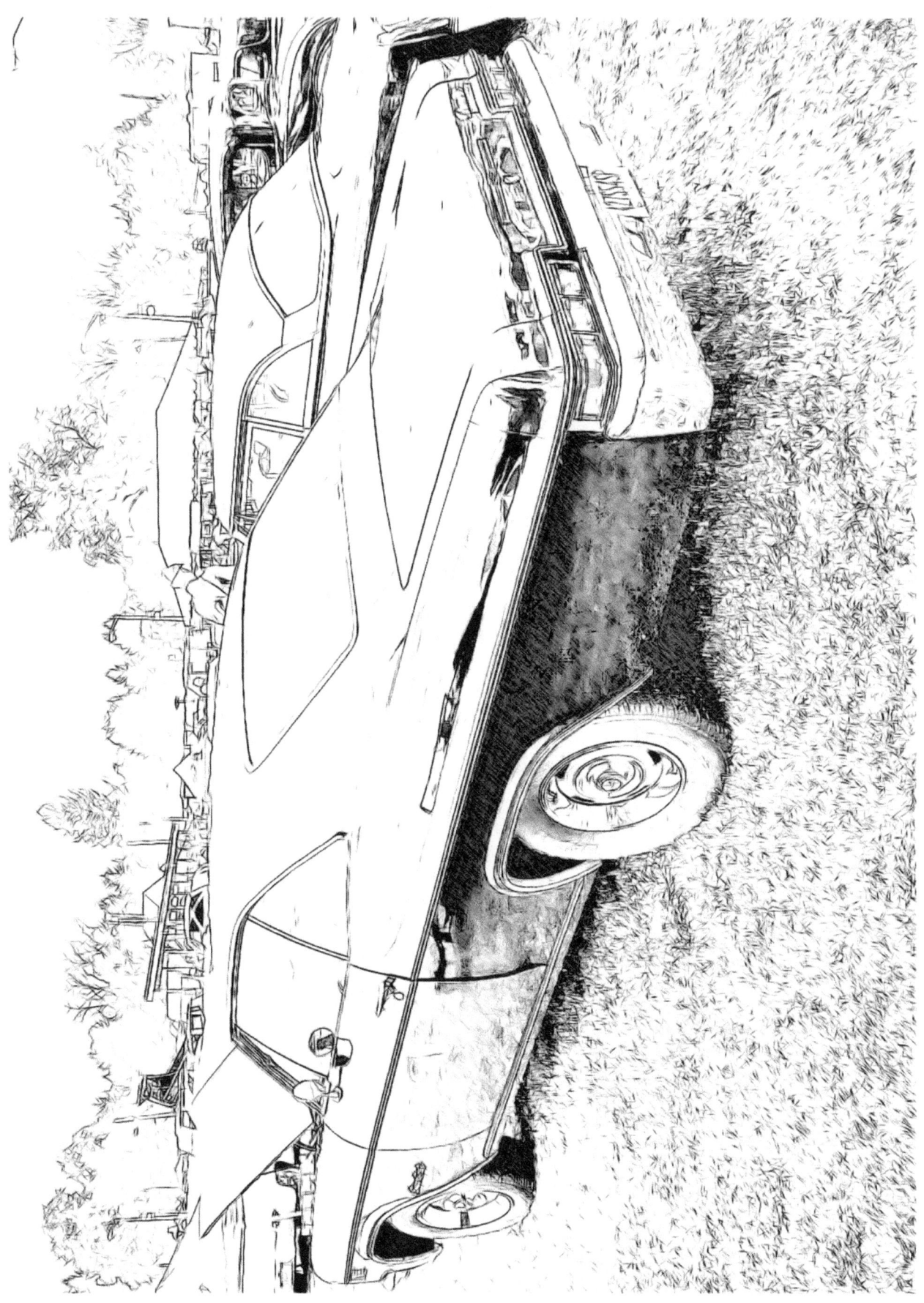

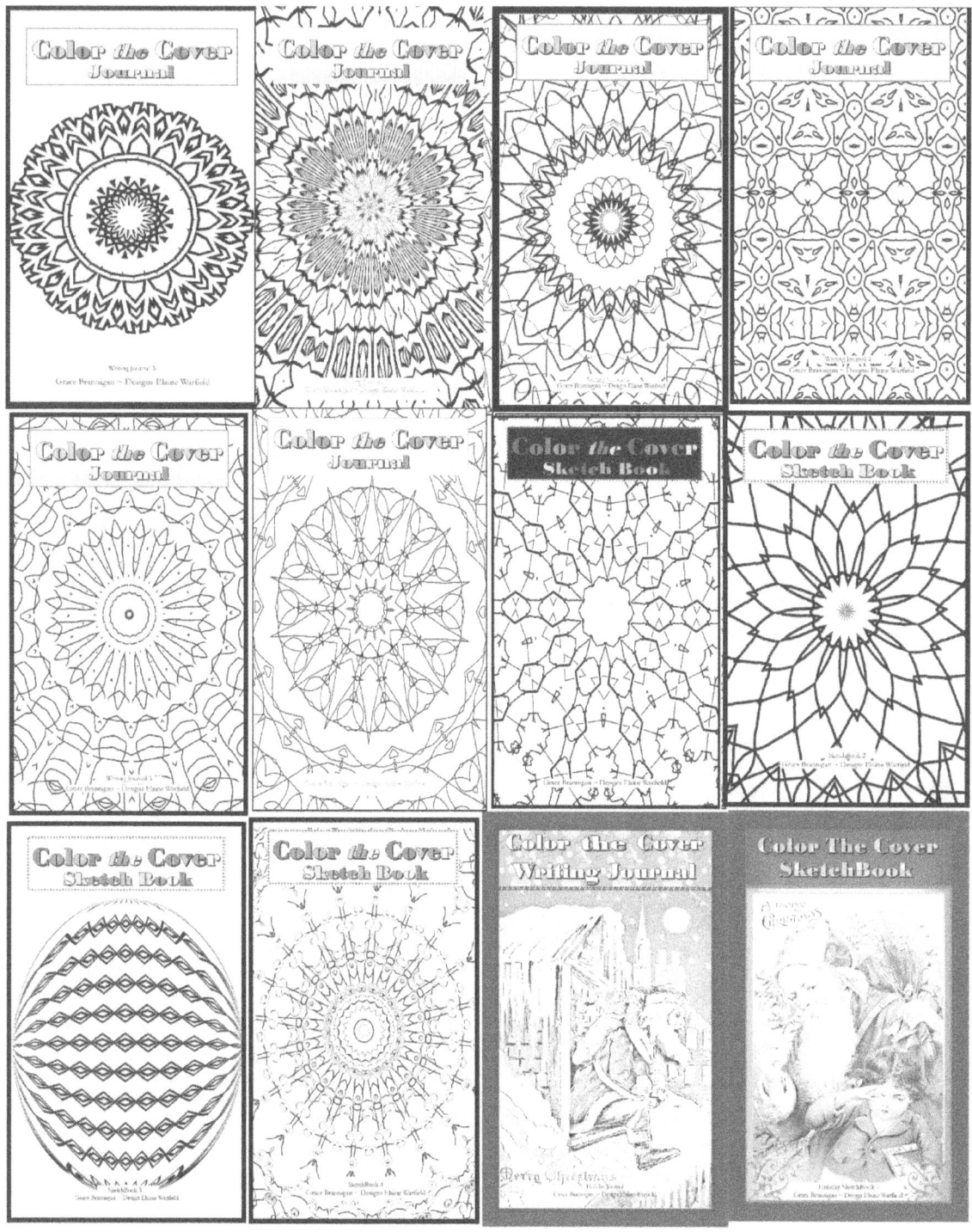

I hope you enjoyed coloring these cars and trucks. Check out the other coloring books in this series! Thank you for purchasing. Please go back to where you bought this book and leave feedback. It really helps the authors and potential buyers. Check out my website for other coloring books!

Facebook: Coloring Books For Adults Info

Website: http://www.ColoringBooksForAdults.info

Twitter: @ColoringAdults